P9-DEA-849

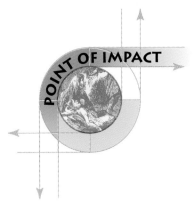

POINT OF IMPACT

The Irish Famine

The Birth of Irish America

TONY ALLAN

Heinemann Library
Chicago, Illinois

J
941.5
A

© 2001 Reed Educational & Professional Publishing
Published by Heinemann Library,
an imprint of Reed Educational & Professional Publishing,
Chicago, IL

Customer Service 888-454-2279

Visit our website at www.heinemannlibrary.com

All rights reserved. No part of this publication may be reproduced or transmitted in any form or by any means, electronic or mechanical, including photocopying, recording, taping, or any information storage and retrieval system, without permission in writing from the publisher.

Produced for Heinemann Library by Discovery Books Limited
Designed by Ian Winton
Illustrations by Stefan Chabluk
Printed in Hong Kong

05 04 03 02 01
10 9 8 7 6 5 4 3 2 1

Library of Congress Cataloging-in-Publication Data

Allan, Tony, 1967–
    The Irish famine : the birth of Irish America / Tony Allan.
        p. cm. -- (Point of impact)
    Includes bibliographical references and index.
    ISBN 1-58810-077-4 (lib. bdg.)
    1. Ireland--History--Famine, 1845-1852--Juvenile literature. 2. Ireland--Emigration
and immigration--Juvenile literature. 3. Irish--Foreign countries--History--Juvenile
literature. 4. Irish Americans--History--Juvenile literature. [1. Ireland--History--Famine,
1845-1852. 2. Ireland--Emigration and immigration. 3. Irish Americans--History.] I.
Title. II. Series.

DA950.7 .A45 2001
941.5081--dc21
                                                    00-046087

Acknowledgments
The Publishers would like to thank the following for permission to reproduce photographs:
Hulton Getty, pp. 4, 9, 19, 21, 22 (and bottom front cover), 27; Illustrated London News, p. 5; Mary Evans Picture Library, pp. 6, 7, 8, 10, 12, 13, 14, 16 (and top front cover), 17, 20, 23, 25, 26, 28; The Art Archive, pp. 11, 15; Corbis, p. 24; Corbis/Jan Butchofsky, p. 29.

Cover photographs reproduced with permission of Hulton Getty and Mary Evans Picture Library.

Every effort has been made to contact copyright holders of any material reproduced in this book. Any omissions will be rectified in subsequent printings if notice is given to the Publisher.

Some words are shown in bold, **like this.** You can find out what they mean by looking in the glossary.

A Note About Dates: In this book, some dates are followed by the letters C.E. (Common Era). This is used instead of the older abbreviation A.D. (*Anno Domini,* which means "in the year of the Lord"). The date numbers are the same in both systems.

Contents

The Great Hunger

A family tragedy

"On Sunday last, 20 December, a young woman begging in the streets of Cork collapsed and was at first unable to move or speak. After being given 'restorations' and taken home to her cabin, she told those helping her that both her mother and father had died in the last fortnight. At the same time she directed their attention to a heap of dirty straw that lay in the corner and apparently concealed some object under it. On removing the covering of straw, the spectators were horrified to behold the corpses of two grown boys. . . . There they had remained for perhaps a week and maybe a fortnight."

In the winter of 1846, the small town of Skibbereen in southwest Ireland saw some of the worst horrors of the Irish Famine. Government inspectors estimated that about 200 people died of hunger in the town in the months of November and December alone.

So wrote a government inspector sent to investigate conditions in western Ireland in December 1846, at the height of the Irish Famine. In its horrific details, his report told of the individual tragedies that lay behind a national calamity. In the small town of Skibbereen alone, he found that 169 people had starved to death in just 3 weeks. In nearby Golleen, so many people were dying that local townspeople devised a coffin with a sliding base. This enabled them to use the same coffin for multiple burials.

The greatest disaster

The famine was, quite simply, the greatest disaster ever to afflict Ireland, and it was all caused by a plant disease. The potato was the staple food of the Irish poor, and when potato **blight** devastated the harvest several years in a row, the consequences were catastrophic. In just five years, it killed a million people and turned Ireland's rapidly expanding population into one that declined for a century.

It also drove even larger numbers abroad. Unable to make a living at home, Irish men and women traveled in tens of thousands to Great Britain and to Canada, often voyaging in overcrowded ships and risking disease. But the greatest number found their way to the United States, where, in the ports of Boston and New York, they laid the foundations of what would one day be a thriving, nationwide Irish-American community.

These pictures from the *Illustrated London News* of August 1846 show a healthy potato plant with an inset showing signs of the potato disease *(Phythophthora infestans)* that caused the Irish famine.

NO LACK OF FOOD?

One of the strangest things about the famine was that food continued to be exported from Ireland throughout the years of hunger. Even in Skibbereen, when hundreds were dying, a local inspector reported that *"On Saturday, notwithstanding all this distress, there was a market plentifully supplied with meat, bread, fish, in short everything."* The problem was not so much a lack of food as the extreme poverty of the poorer people, who had no money to buy the supplies that were available.

Rulers and Rebels

A troubled land

Although unmatched in its horror, the famine was just one in a series of tragedies that has dotted Ireland's history. The island had known a time of greatness in the troubled period after the collapse of the Roman Empire (5th–9th centuries C.E.), when its monks and artists helped keep European civilization alive. But politically it was split between warring kingdoms, and these divisions would prove to be Ireland's undoing.

The English connection

In 1171, King Henry II of England took advantage of Irish feuding to claim control over the island, and from that time on Ireland's destiny was linked with that of England. But unlike Scotland and Wales, which came to accept English rule, Ireland never willingly accepted the relationship.

One problem was distance—Ireland was cut off from England by the Irish Sea. Lawmakers in London rarely concerned themselves with Irish interests. Language was another problem, for until the early 19th century most Irish people spoke **Gaelic** rather than English. Finally, religious upheavals of the 16th century caused the most lasting rift between Ireland and England. When the pope forbade Henry VIII to divorce his first wife, the king left Catholicism and started his own church. Loyal subjects were expected to join. Ireland stayed Roman **Catholic**.

England's Protestant King William III led his men against a Catholic Irish army at the Battle of the Boyne in 1690. William's victory set the scene for the "Protestant Ascendancy," a period of more than a century in which Irish Catholics saw many of their civil rights taken away.

Divided loyalties

At a time when most wars were fought over religion, this split had ominous implications. In foreign affairs, Catholic Ireland's sympathies lay with other Catholic countries, who were often **Protestant** England's enemies.

To solve this problem Queen Elizabeth I (1533–1603) began encouraging English and Scottish Protestants to settle in Ireland by giving them grants of land. These Protestant settlements caused bitterness and helped stir up a series of armed revolts that were put down with much bloodshed. In 1690, a significant uprising by Irish Catholics in support of the deposed English king, James II, was crushed by William III, who was also known as William of Orange, at the Battle of the Boyne. The conflict divides the Irish to this day—many Northern Irish Protestants still call themselves Orangemen to honor William's cause.

This is an artist's rendering of a peasant rebels' camp at Vinegar Hill in County Wexford during a 1798 uprising against British rule. In the course of the revolt, which was put down quickly by government troops, a dozen captured Protestants were put to death (shown at left).

The Act of Union

The final stage in England's takeover of Ireland followed another unsuccessful uprising in 1798. By the Act of Union of 1801, Ireland lost her own parliament and became subject to direct rule from London as part of the United Kingdom of Great Britain and Ireland.

After the Act, calm seemingly settled on Ireland, but appearances were deceptive. Under the surface, tensions simmered. Ireland was a divided society. People were divided over many issues, including religion, language, and wealth.

The Two Irelands

The humiliation of the penal laws

After the **Catholic** defeat at the Battle of the Boyne, Ireland's religious divisions were written into law. The victorious **Protestants** forced through a series of measures collectively known as the **penal laws.** These made it illegal for any Catholic to hold office, stand for Parliament, vote, join the armed forces, or attend any British university. Worse still, Catholics were not allowed to buy land. Those who already owned it had to subdivide their estates on the death of the head of the family between all the surviving children—unless any converted to Protestantism, in which case they got it all.

The Protestant Ascendancy

The result of these measures was that by the late 18th century Catholics, who made up the bulk of the population, owned less than five percent of Ireland's land. All the rest belonged to Protestants who often lived in magnificent style. Their wealth can still be seen in the splendid mansions they constructed across the Irish countryside and in their elegant town houses in Dublin.

A mansion in County Wicklow suggests the grand manner in which the wealthy landowners of the Protestant Ascendancy lived. The Ascendancy also spawned a dazzling culture, graced by writers like Jonathan Swift, author of *Gulliver's Travels,* and the playwright Richard Brinsley Sheridan.

Scraping by

For the rest of the population, though, the situation was very different. Although a few wealthy landowning families survived, most Catholics had to scrape along as best they could. Most rented land from Protestant landlords, who tended to see them not as tenants to whom they had responsibilities, as in England, but simply as sources of income. Feeling ill at ease among their **Gaelic**-speaking tenants, few big landowners chose to spend much time on their estates, preferring to lead comfortable lives in Dublin or London instead.

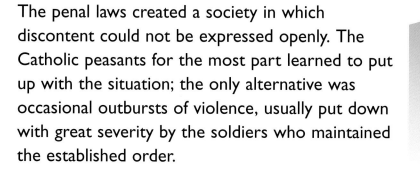

A mother in the town of Clonakilty, near Skibbereen, begs for money to buy a coffin to bury her dead baby.

The penal laws created a society in which discontent could not be expressed openly. The Catholic peasants for the most part learned to put up with the situation; the only alternative was occasional outbursts of violence, usually put down with great severity by the soldiers who maintained the established order.

PEASANT REBELS

With no political voice to speak for them, Irish peasants joined secret societies to protect their interests. A Frenchman touring Ireland in 1796 described such groups at work: *"They assembled at night in great numbers in certain parts of Ireland, and in order that they might recognize each other safely, they wore their shirts outside their clothes, from whence came the name of 'White Boys.' In this garb they overran the country, breaking the doors and gates of [their targets'] houses, and if they could catch the [landowners'] cattle they mutilated them by cutting off their tails and ears. All the time they did no other violent act, and a traveler might have gone through the country with perfect security."*

The Scourge of Poverty

Poverty and the penal laws

The most obvious effect of the social system that developed out of the **penal laws** was that much of

the population lived in deep poverty. There were corners of prosperity, most notably in the northeastern province of Ulster, which was inhabited largely by **Protestant** settlers from Scotland. A linen industry developed there in the late 18th century and began to flourish.

Workers prepare linen at a textile mill in County Down in 1783. There was little industrial production in Ireland before the Famine, and what there was became concentrated in the northeastern province of Ulster.

An underdeveloped land

For the most part, though, industrialization was something Ireland knew little about. It did not have the coal and iron that fueled the manufacturing revolution then under way in mainland Britain. And the social system in Ireland did little to encourage the people to improve things. The countryside remained underdeveloped—by 1848, there were about 5,000 miles of railroad track in Britain as a whole, but only 375 miles in Ireland.

For the **Catholic** majority scraping a living off the land, conditions were often appalling. Those who owned their own farms worked ever-smaller holdings as the land was continually subdivided. Yet they were better off than most of the population, forced to rent small plots, often on one-year **conacre** leases that allowed them to be **evicted** for almost any reason.

Even so, because of the demand for land in a country with few other jobs, rents were ruinously high—almost double those in England.

Life on the bottom

The result was the lowest standard of living in Europe. The 1841 **census** revealed that nearly half of all families in the countryside were living in single-room mud cabins without windows; in parts of western Ireland, it was closer to three-fifths. Yet even these makeshift homes were not the bottom of the heap; tenants who were evicted or laborers without land were reduced to putting roofs over ditches or living in holes burrowed into dirt mounds. The Duke of Wellington, the one-time prime minister of Britain as well as an Irish landowner himself, knew what he was talking about when he told the House of Lords in 1838 that *"there never was a country in which poverty existed to the extent it exists in Ireland."*

LIVING ON THE EDGE
Throughout most of Ireland, furniture was a luxury that few could afford. A survey of the village of Tullahobagly in County Donegal in 1837 revealed that its 9,000 inhabitants had a total of only 10 beds, 93 chairs, and 243 stools. Most people slept and ate on the beaten-earth floors of their shacks.

A farmer's wife serves a meal in a poor cabin. Furniture was a luxury for most Irish people at the time.

The Potato to the Rescue

The potato feeds a nation

In the terrible social conditions of the early 19th century, much of Ireland survived on a single crop: the potato. Originally introduced by **Protestant** settlers, it had spread across the nation in the 18th century, partly because it was useful in breaking up the land for sowing grain.

A healthy diet

Soon, though, it won popularity in its own right. It was easy to grow and was highly productive: a little more than an acre of land, planted with potatoes, could feed a family of six, where grain would have required five times as much land. The potato was also nutritious. Many Irish people of all ages survived on a potato diet, balanced by some dairy products, salt, and cabbage. The same visitors who were shocked by the abject poverty of rural Ireland were often surprised to see how healthy many of the poor farmers and their families appeared to be.

In good times, even poor families could live quite well if, like this one, they had a store of potatoes in the loft and some pigs and poultry to provide meat and eggs to supplement the diet.

The result was that across much of the country people became increasingly dependent on the potato. Typically, people consumed several pounds of potatoes every day, all year round. Nothing was wasted. Peelings and potatoes too small for cooking were fed to poultry or pigs, which could be fattened and sold to pay the rent. The pig manure went to fertilize the potato fields.

Some regions became more dependent on the potato than others. In the "oatmeal zones" of Ulster and northern Leinster, even the poor could usually supplement their diet with oats. But in large parts of southern and western Ireland, the potato was the only significant food.

The risks of dependence

People were aware at the time of the dangers of over-dependence on a single crop. For all their benefits, potatoes did not keep well, and could not be stored from one season to the next. There had even been crop failures in the past, but they had generally been localized and short-lived. In general, the potato had proved less prone to bad harvests than cereal crops.

Most of all, there was simply no alternative to the potato, and so the nation's reliance on it grew. By 1845, an estimated one and a half million **landless** laborers and their families depended on it almost entirely, and for another three million it was the main food. If people did think of an Ireland without potatoes, they quickly put the thought out of their minds—the prospect was just too terrible for them to consider.

The failure of the potato harvest threatened the survival of peasants such as this man and his daughter, whose homes were little more than shacks. They would be among the first to suffer from such a calamity.

More Mouths to Feed

An exploding population

The situation in the 1840s was the more dangerous because Ireland had experienced a population explosion over the previous 100 years. In 1741 there had been fewer than 2,500,000 Irish, but by 1800 the number had doubled, and it continued to rise. The 1841 **census** recorded more than eight million people, and even that figure was thought to be too low. Britain's future prime minister Benjamin Disraeli declared Ireland to be the most densely populated country in the whole of Europe.

The hungry millions

At first sight it seems odd that the population should have risen in the face of intense poverty, but in fact the two factors went together, much as they do in the world's poorest countries today. It was actually among the **landless** peasants that the rate of population growth was highest. While Irish farmers tended to wait until their thirties before getting married, carefully saving to be able to afford the expense, the very poor had no such worries. For them, saving up money was unnecessary. A couple could leave their own families' crowded mud cabins and build one of their own for next to nothing in a matter of days. Having no possessions to begin with, they expected none after marriage. Asked why the poor married so young, a **Catholic** bishop in 1835 replied, *"They cannot be worse off than they are, and they may help each other."*

Farm laborers who had made the trip to England to help with the harvest line up for places on the boat back to Ireland. Seasonal work overseas helped ease the burden of unemployment at home.

Support in old age

Typically, poor couples married at sixteen or seventeen and went on to have large families. They had every reason for doing so; in a society without pensions, children were a couple's only hope of support in old age.

Even so, the growing numbers drained the resources of the country. Many parents, unable to feed all their children, sent some to Dublin, where the population increased by 400% between 1700 and 1800. Yet the pressure on the land still increased. Areas on mountainsides and in bogs were cultivated to feed the new mouths, and existing agricultural land was further subdivided to provide ever smaller parcels of land for families to farm.

But ultimately all the growth depended on the availability of a cheap food supply, and that meant the potato. In 1845, this basic staple was suddenly threatened in a totally unexpected way.

The elegance of Sackville Street in the heart of Dublin was a far cry from the city's teeming slums, where most of the population lived. One observer of these reported: "I have frequently surprised from ten to sixteen persons, of all ages and sexes, in a room not fifteen feet square, stretched on a wad of filthy straw swarming with vermin."

First Signs of Trouble

The potato blight

The disaster that struck Ireland in the autumn of 1845 was a new disease: the potato **blight.** Its symptoms were black spots on the upper leaves of the plant and a white mold underneath. The potatoes themselves often looked wholesome on the outside, but the insides quickly turned to a stinking mush. The blight flourished in mild, damp weather, leading scientists at the time to consider it a form of wet rot. In fact, it was a fungus whose spores were spread by wind and insects, rapidly affecting entire districts.

The blight had first appeared in the United States in 1843, reaching continental Europe in the spring of 1845, probably through shipments of infected seeds. At first, Ireland seemed to have been spared; the early crop in August was excellent. But when the late harvest was gathered in October, at least a third of the potatoes were found to be affected.

DISCOVERING THE BLIGHT

A wealthy farmer described the experience of discovering the blight when it reached central Ireland: *"On August 6, 1846—I shall not readily forget the day—I rode up as usual to my mountain property, and my feelings may be imagined when before I saw the crop, I smelt the fearful stench... [Before long] the luxuriant stalks withered, the leaves decayed, the disease extended to the tubers, and the stench from the rotting of such an immense amount of rich vegetable matter became almost intolerable."*

A family struggles to come to terms with the failure of their potato crop. No one at the time had any doubts that starvation threatened if the blight turned the potatoes rotten.

A sense of crisis

No one at the time doubted the seriousness of the situation. The government in London, headed by Sir Robert Peel, acted quickly to help. A relief commission was set up in Dublin to coordinate the activities of some 650 local committees established to provide famine relief. A system of **public works** was also financed by the government so that work could be given to the unemployed to help with beneficial projects like road building. An English civil servant named Charles Trevelyan, the head of the Treasury, was given the job of supervising the relief effort from London.

Although never popular in Ireland, the Conservative prime minister Sir Robert Peel in fact took firm action to lessen the first effects of the famine.

Peel went further, secretly authorizing the purchase of a large quantity of corn from the United States. He never intended to give this directly to the hungry; instead, it was to be kept in government depots and released onto the market if food prices rose too high, preventing **profiteering.** In 1846 Peel repealed the Corn Laws to cut the price of corn, but it still remained too expensive for the Irish poor.

Peel's measures could not prevent suffering in Ireland—there was terrible hunger and an epidemic of **typhus** fever. Even so, he left office after a general election in 1846 knowing that at least no one had died of starvation alone during his time as prime minister. Worse was to follow in the years to come.

The Terrible Winter

A time of foreboding

The summer of 1846 was a time of foreboding in Ireland. Even in good times, these were the "hungry months" when one potato crop was exhausted and the next had yet to be harvested. Now there was the fear that, with the country's reserves already exhausted, the new crop would be diseased too.

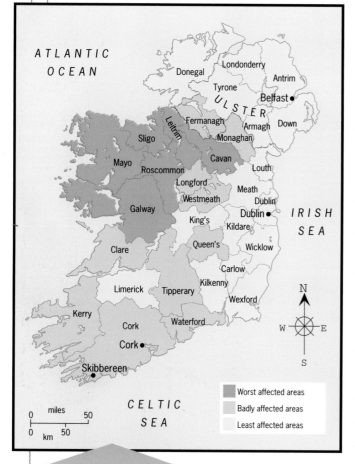

ATLANTIC OCEAN

Donegal
Londonderry
Antrim
Tyrone
Belfast
ULSTER
Fermanagh
Armagh
Down
Leitrim
Sligo
Monaghan
Cavan
Mayo
Roscommon
Louth
Longford
Meath
Westmeath
Dublin
Galway
Dublin
IRISH SEA
King's
Kildare
Queen's
Wicklow
Clare
Carlow
Kilkenny
Limerick
Tipperary
Wexford
Kerry
Waterford
Cork
Cork
Skibbereen
CELTIC SEA

■	Worst affected areas
■	Badly affected areas
□	Least affected areas

miles 0 50
km 0 50

N W E S

While most of Ireland suffered from the effects of the potato famine, the worst hit areas were in the west and south of the country.

There was also a fresh government in London, under the leadership of Lord John Russell. He chose to leave Charles Trevelyan at his post as the famine relief coordinator, and that summer Trevelyan made a fateful decision. Fearing above all to increase the burden on British taxpayers, he decided not to buy any more grain reserves.

The blight returns

In Ireland, people's worst fears were soon realized. A warm, wet summer provided ideal conditions for the **blight** to spread. By August it was apparent that the potato crop would be disastrously affected; in fact, nine-tenths was eventually lost.

Only government action on a massive scale could have prevented calamity, but the government did almost nothing. It believed that **market forces** should be left to work, which meant leaving the economy to run as it always had, even allowing exports of grain from Ireland to continue. Relief

SAVING MONEY, NOT LIVES

Even when the full scale of the tragedy became apparent, Trevelyan remained more concerned about saving money than saving lives. While admitting in a private letter that *"This is a real famine, in which thousands and thousands of people are likely to die,"* he went on to insist, *"If the Irish once find out there are any circumstances in which they can get free government grants, we shall have a system of mendicancy [begging] such as the world never saw."*

of the starving was left principally to local landowners, even though they had already shown themselves for the most part unwilling to shoulder the burden.

Famine fever

The result was hunger on a devastating scale, and in its wake came disease. In their weakened condition, famine victims fell prey to horrific and often fatal diseases such as **typhus,** yellow fever, and dysentery. Shocked eyewitnesses described whole villages where much of the population lay sick and starving on the floors of their cabins, listless with "famine fever."

For those of the **destitute** who could still help themselves, there was only the remnants of Peel's system of **public works.** There were never enough jobs to go around, even though wages were kept at near-starvation levels so as not to undercut other sources of employment. Worse still, wages were often paid late. As the terrible winter of 1846 to 1847 wore on, reports of deaths of workers on public works projects became common.

At the height of the famine, a mother and son search despairingly in a field of stubble for potatoes fit to eat. Faced with starvation, families would often eat rotten and stinking potatoes that they would normally not even have fed to their animals.

Why Was More Not Done to Help?

Aid for the victims

Many millions of people in Ireland, Great Britain, and other countries around the world were appalled by the famine and did everything in their power to help the victims. In Ireland, good landowners waived rents and provided work for the **destitute** and food for the hungry. In England, a charity called the British Association raised nearly £500,000—worth about $37,500,000 in today's dollars. Queen Victoria herself gave £2,000. Similar amounts were raised in the U.S., where Congress made warships available to transport food. Over 100 cargoes arrived in 1847 alone.

The U.S. frigate *Macedonian* docks at Cork in July 1847, bringing food donated in response to famine appeals. The U.S. government loaned two naval vessels to carry the supplies to Ireland.

Setting up soup kitchens

In Ireland itself, some of the most effective work was done by the **Quakers,** who set up **soup kitchens** in distressed areas from November 1846 on. These proved so successful that they eventually shamed the British government into a short-lived change of heart. In January 1847, the relief coordinators discontinued the previous system of **public works** and instead opened soup kitchens of their own, substantially reducing the number of deaths over the summer months. But the kitchens were considered too expensive to be more than a temporary measure. By autumn, they were closed—to fatal effect.

An act of God?

The fact was that throughout the crisis, only the government could have mobilized the resources needed to avert disaster, and it failed to take sufficient action. There was no established tradition of government intervention in Ireland. Tragedies like the famine were regarded at the time as calamities sent by God, about which little could be done. When famine had wiped out a tenth of the Irish population a century before, no action at all had been taken. Many people believed that the deaths, however tragic, were in the long run the only possible solution to overpopulation and poverty.

Market forces

Most important in the minds of people like Charles Trevelyan, though, were ideas of political economy. In their view, markets worked best when left to themselves. They thought that the growing demand for food in Ireland would create new sources of supply. Thus, any attempt by government to intervene could only do harm. But while their ideas might have made sense in a developed economy like England's, they could never have worked in Ireland. There, even in good times, millions of people had no money. In such extreme conditions, notions of a market economy became meaningless.

Workers prepare food for the hungry in a soup kitchen run by the Quakers, a charitably-minded religious group. Throughout the famine, privately-run relief efforts were more effective than government programs in bringing help to the needy.

A Way Out over the Seas

The emigration option

As people realized the full horror of what was happening, they sought a way out through **emigration.** There was already a tradition of Irish people traveling to North America—about a million had gone in the 30 years before 1845. In 1846, at the start of the famine, 51,752 people emigrated to the United States. By 1847 this figure had more than doubled. In 1851, emigration reached its peak, with 221,253 Irish men, women, and children making the sea journey.

Emigrants seeking a better life abroad wait on the dockside at Cork to embark for the United States or Canada. The prospect of the journey often was terrifying for the Irish, many of whom had never before traveled more than 30 miles from their homes.

Many others who left Ireland never got beyond Britain, where the poorer emigrants went to earn the money for the transatlantic voyage by casual labor—a process known as "step migration." By 1847, the streets of Liverpool, Glasgow, and other cities were full of starving people.

The transatlantic crossing

Of those who did make the crossing, many went to Canada, then a British colony. The reasons were economic—fares were cheap on the Canadian timber ships, which offered passages at low prices to fill their empty holds for the return journey.

Conditions on board were mostly appalling. Passengers were normally expected to take food with them for the journey, but few then could afford that luxury. Hunger, overcrowding, and shortages of water and sanitary facilities turned the ships into breeding grounds for disease. Many thousands of emigrants who set sail died on the voyage.

The final destination of most emigrants was the United States. Even among those who sailed for Canada, many subsequently sought to cross the border. U.S. authorities avoided the worst of the shipborne epidemics by demanding higher standards of hygiene on board vessels docking at U.S. ports. By 1848, regulations were tightened in Canada also, and the worst of the "ocean plague," as it became known, was over.

The empty land

But the human outflow continued, sometimes financed by landowners eager to clear their lands of unwanted tenants. By 1850, some districts of Ireland were becoming depopulated. Entire families—sometimes even whole villages—had gone in search of better prospects across the seas, thousands of miles from the country they still thought of as home.

A COLD WELCOME
An eyewitness who traveled in one of the 1847 "coffin ships" described the scene at Grosse Isle, the Canadian **quarantine** station outside Quebec, when the sick were taken to shore in boats: *"Hundreds were literally flung on the beach, left amid the mud and stones to crawl on the dry land as best they could."* Even so, most were glad to get to land; the vessel had been moored off the island for a week, without medical help or fresh water.

Conditions on board the transatlantic "coffin ships" of 1847 were as bad as anything in Ireland itself. **Typhus** fever spread in the overcrowded hulks, killing many thousands of those who made the voyage.

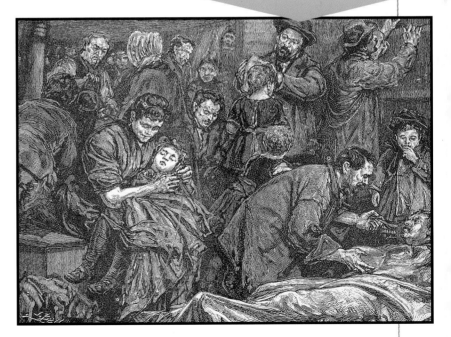

A New Life in a New Land

The shock of arrival

For the millions who found their way across the Atlantic, life at first was little better than it had been in Ireland. On arrival in Boston and especially New York, they fell victim to swindlers who regularly cheated new arrivals out of the few possessions they had managed to save.

Even though most **immigrants** came from the countryside, they preferred to stay in the ports where they first landed to be among other Irish. They ended up living in some of the worst slums in the United States, often cramming ten or more people into a room.

Unwanted guests

They also encountered much hostility from their unwilling hosts. Americans had shown great generosity in contributing to relief funds for famine victims in Ireland; but when the poor and starving turned up on their own doorstep, they saw the newcomers as a threat. First and foremost, there were well-founded fears of the diseases the Irish brought with them. It was well-known that Montreal in Canada had suffered a **typhus** epidemic following the first wave of immigration.

Living conditions for many Irish immigrants did not improve in the new country. They often found themselves living in the slums.

A VIOLENT UNDERCLASS

In the early famine years, the cities of Boston and New York, where most immigrants landed, reeled under the impact of the social problems caused by the jobless newcomers. In the five years prior to 1848, Boston police reported increases of 266 percent in murders, 1,700 percent in attempts to kill, and 465 percent in armed assaults. In addition, 1,500 children below the age of 16 were said to be begging in the streets.

Unwelcome workers

There were also worries that the low pay for which the unskilled immigrants were prepared to work would undercut American workers' wages. In 1844, even before the famine **emigration** got under way, there had been anti-Irish riots in Philadelphia that left thirteen dead. In fact the first-generation immigrants usually ended up doing the hard, dangerous, and ill-paid jobs that no one else wanted. Much of the U.S. transportation infrastructure of roads, railroads, and canals was built in the nineteenth century by Irish laborers.

In time, though, the newcomers learned to take advantage of the opportunities offered by the new land. As the Irish-American community took root, it became richer and more respected. Meanwhile, fresh waves of immigrants from other lands took the place the Irish had once occupied at the bottom of the economic ladder.

Workers lay track for the transcontinental railroad, which eventually linked the eastern United States with California and the Pacific Ocean. Much of the hard work of building U.S. railroads was done by Irish laborers.

The Ordeal Is Slow Ending

The suffering continues

For those who stayed behind in Ireland, the suffering continued. By 1848 times were hard in Great Britain too, and the government's overriding concern was to save money. With the closing of the **soup kitchens,** the only option for the **destitute** was to seek places in the workhouses. These were prison-like institutions that provided food and shelter in return for unpaid labor. That year saw a surge in the numbers of applicants. Even so, the government in London decided that the extra cost should be borne almost entirely by Ireland alone.

Homeless and helpless

Unable to pay their rent, members of a family are locked out of their home. Some tenants evicted by landlords ended up dying in the streets.

The result was a huge rise in **rates** that ended up **bankrupting** many smaller landowners, who were themselves then forced to join the lines at the workhouse doors. Another effect was to dramatically increase the number of **evictions,** as landlords sought to get rid of poor tenants whose rates they were expected to pay. In 1850, more than 100,000 people were driven from their homes.

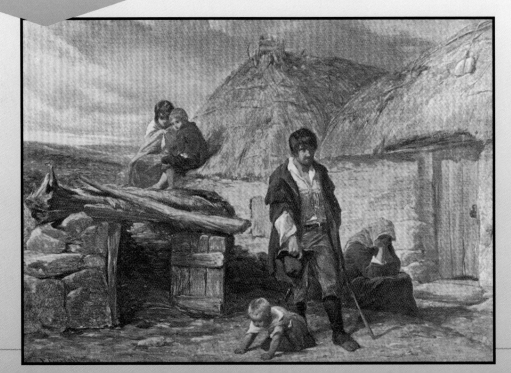

Within the workhouses themselves, conditions were often appalling. Disease was rampant, with cholera added to other epidemics after 1848. In early 1849, as many as 2,500 people were dying each week in the institutions that were supposed to support them.

WORKHOUSE LIFE

Sidney Osborne, a clergyman who set out to expose the conditions in Irish workhouses, wrote the following about one in the town of Limerick: *"I have no words with which I can give any real idea of the sad condition of the inmates of two large yards at the parent house, in which were a very large number of young female children; many of them were clothed in the merest dirty rags; they were in the dirt collected on their persons for many weeks; there was not the slightest evidence of the least care being taken of them."*

Counting the cost

There was no clear-cut end to the famine. When its effects did fade from 1850 on, it was mainly because death and **emigration** had reduced the pressure on resources. The size of the calamity it had wrought was revealed in the national **census** of 1851. Ireland's population, which would otherwise have been over 9 million, had fallen to 6.6 million. About 1.5 million Irish men, women, and children had been forced to emigrate. The others had died of hunger or disease.

Starving peasants mob the gates of a workhouse in search of food. Despite their grim and forbidding nature, these prison-like institutions at least provided meals and shelter, and people fought for places in them.

An Enduring Legacy of Bitterness

The effects of the famine

The famine affected the destiny of more than one nation. In Ireland itself, it had long-lasting social and cultural effects. In the countryside, the number of **smallholdings** was drastically reduced and the practice of subdividing farms came to an end. Potato-growing and crop-raising generally gave way to sheep- and cattle-rearing. The use of **Gaelic** also fell away. It had been the native language of almost half the population before the catastrophe, but so many Gaelic-speakers died or emigrated that it never really recovered. However, a recent revival in the use of Gaelic has kept the language alive.

In the wake of the famine and the **emigration** that followed, whole villages in western Ireland became deserted. Even today, the population of Ireland as a whole is less than six million—well below its pre-famine level.

The wider effects on Ireland were just as enduring. Before the famine, the nation's population of over eight million was nearly half that of Great Britain. Afterwards it continued to shrink, so that in 1951, a century after the famine ended, it stood at just 4,250,000—half its pre-famine level, and by that time less than one-tenth that of Great Britain. Only in recent decades has the Irish population begun to expand, as increasing wealth has made Ireland once more a land of opportunity.

Calls for independence

Politically, the lasting effect of the tragedy was a sense of bitterness toward the British government that had done so little to help. For some, the anger took a violent form. **Catholic** opposition to rule from London, which had previously been peaceful, turned to direct confrontation with the founding of the **Fenian** movement, devoted to the revolutionary overthrow of British rule. A direct line of violent protest links the famine years to the establishment of the Irish Free State in 1921 and the Republic of Ireland in 1949.

Birth of a community

But the effects were also felt overseas, and above all in the United States, where the Irish underclass of the 1840s and 1850s merged into the American mainstream without ever losing its cultural roots. By the 20th century, Irish-Americans had more than claimed their share of the American dream, ranking among the most prosperous of all **immigrant** groups.

The success of the community as a whole was reflected even more dramatically in that of individual families. Among the thousands of Irish immigrants who died of fever on arrival in North America in 1847 was a certain Mrs. Ford, whose grandson Henry was to create the world's most famous automobile empire. Famine immigrants from the Irish counties of Wexford and Kerry founded the family dynasty that produced John F. Kennedy, 35th President of the United States.

This is a statue of Annie Moore and her brothers, some of the first Irish immigrants to reach the United States during the potato famine. They hoped for a better life after the hunger and poverty of Ireland.

Important Dates

1171		Henry II claims overlordship of Ireland
1534		England breaks with Rome. Henry VIII establishes the Church of England. Ireland remains Roman **Catholic.**
1584		Elizabeth I seizes land in Munster for English settlement
1610		Large-scale **Protestant** settlement of Ulster begins
1690		William of Orange defeats Catholics at the Battle of the Boyne
1692		Catholics excluded from Irish parliament. First **penal laws** passed.
1741		Famine kills one-tenth of Irish population
1798		United Irishmen launch unsuccessful uprising
1801		Act of Union links Britain and Ireland in United Kingdom
1838		Poor Law establishes network of 130 workhouses across Ireland
1841		**Census** numbers Irish population at 8,175,124
1843		Potato **blight** first appears in the United States
1845	**September**	First signs of potato blight in Ireland
	November	Charles Trevelyan takes charge of famine relief operations
1846	**July**	Lord John Russell becomes British prime minister
	November	**Quakers** set up first **soup kitchens**
1847	**January**	British Association formed to raise money for famine victims
	January	Soup Kitchen Act authorizes state-run soup kitchens
	May	First fever cases reach Grosse Isle in Canada
	June	Poor Law Extension Act—Irish taxpayers must meet cost of workhouses
	September	Declaring famine over, government closes soup kitchens
1848		Total failure of potato crop makes famine worse
1849		Queen Victoria visits Ireland
1850		**Evictions** reach a peak, with 100,000 made homeless
1851		Census shows Irish population has dropped to 6,552,385
1921		Irish Free State established—Ulster remains linked to Britain
1949		Republic of Ireland officially proclaimed
1961		John F. Kennedy, descendant of Irish **immigrants,** becomes first Catholic president of United States

Glossary

bankrupt   in a state of financial ruin

blight   disease of plants

Catholic   member of the Roman Catholic Church, whose supreme leader is the pope

census   official count of the population

conacre   farmland rented for a single season

destitute   without money or the means to make any

emigration   leaving one's own country to make a new home in a foreign land

evict   to turn tenants out of their homes

Fenian   member of any of various 19th-century Irish revolutionary organizations dedicated to ending British rule

Gaelic   native language of the Celtic people of Ireland

immigrant   person arriving in a new country where he or she wishes to settle

landless   owning no land

market forces   relationship between demand for goods and services and their supply. For a government to leave a situation to market forces means that the government will not intervene, believing that demand will automatically lead to a greater supply.

penal laws   laws passed in Ireland in the 17th and 18th centuries to restrict the rights of Catholics

profiteering   taking advantage of a desperate situation to make excessive profits

Protestant   Christian who is not a member of the Roman Catholic Church

public works   government-financed projects designed to provide jobs for the unemployed

Quaker   member of the Society of Friends, a Christian movement known for its charitable work

quarantine   to place people who have an infectious disease in isolation for a time in order to stop the spread of the disease

rates   tax based on the value of property

smallholding   piece of agricultural land that is smaller than a farm

soup kitchen   place where free food is provided for the needy

typhus   bacterial disease with symptoms of high fever, headaches, and a dark red rash

More Books to Read

Cavan, Seamus. *The Irish-American Experience*. Brookfield, Conn.: Millbrook Press, 1993.

Coffey, Michael, ed. and Terry Golway. *The Irish in America*. New York: Hyperion, 1997.

Connor, Ellwood. *I Am Irish American*. New York: Rosen Publishing Group, Inc., 1997.

Index